THE ART OF
ASS KICKING

THE ART OF
ASS KICKING

WRITTEN BY:

RICK MELLO

authorHOUSE®

AuthorHouse™
1663 Liberty Drive
Bloomington, IN 47403
www.authorhouse.com
Phone: 1 (800) 839-8640

Published by AuthorHouse 02/08/2016

ISBN: 978-1-4969-0945-9 (sc)

FOREWORD

After 70 years of life I felt I needed to express my thoughts on the sport that is my first love, and also to thank all the people who helped me learn, who gave of their valuable time so that I could achieve a better me, and therefore find my calling for the short time the Lord will allow me on this earth. A special thanks to my good friend Vincent (Vinnie) Hines Sr. His knowledge was priceless when we ventured together with our World Champion, Kelsey Jeffries. Two people, whom I never met, also deserve thanks and recognition as they inspired me in life: Willie Pep, former Featherweight Champion of the world, and the late great, Ted Williams, the best hitter in Baseball from 1939-1962. Their accomplishments were and are, amazing, and serve as an inspiration to their sport. To all the people who have passed my way, regardless of the relationship, because some were bad, but mostly they were good ones. God bless you all.

The information I have written is for trainers and boxers, and I will alternate between the two throughout the book. If you are a trainer or a boxer this will help you get ready for the world of boxing, whether amateur or pro.

Rick Mello, 2007

THE ART OF
ASS KICKING

Ted Williams once said that the hardest thing to do in sports was hit a baseball. I guess he never tried to hit Willie Pep. I say hitting Willie Pep would be the second hardest thing to do, the first thing being: trying to not get hit with a left jab on your nose. Let's talk about Willie first. Willie Pep had the best left jab I ever saw. He could throw it from angles that most boxers today don't even know exist. People look at me funny when I say that, because it requires a natural ability, balance and great fitness to do it right! More so than any other sport. What you are trying to do is to be able to throw a jab from any angle with lightening speed and thundering force, and hit your opponent with effect. Let's turn to Ted Williams for a moment,

He had the greatest rotation of his upper body when swinging at a baseball that I ever saw. He got his legs and his hips, sholders, arms and wrist into the bat, which generated such great bat speed, which in turn created such force when he made contact with the ball and made it look like lighting coming of the end of the bat. The motion that I saw hundreds of times I copied and made it fit into my style of throwing punches. It worked magic when I got it down perfect. I'll explain later in this manuscript. Note: Williams retired with a 347 batting average. He could with uncanny accuracy hit a ball coming in at him from different angles.

Boxing has been crying for good boxers for years, but the trouble is there ain't any good trainers around anymore who teach a boxer the several ways to throw a jab. Jabbing is a lost art, and not being taught properly because all the good teachers are all gone. Currently, at every level of boxing, it's being taught incorrectly or worse, not at all. Everybody thinks they know how to jab, but they really don't. After sixty years in the game as a boxer, and trainer, I'm convinced by what I see: that there aren't many good jabbing boxers who can stick a guy and ring his bell, or better still, control a fight. Where's the finesse?

I've heard for years that boxing is a dead sport because of a few deaths that have appeared on television. Bullshit! What *is* "dead" are the trainers, officials, and the boxers from the neck up. It all starts with the trainer, and if he does not train the fighter from the feet up, he should find another sport that trains from the neck down. I think boxing would improve as a sport if the trainers were re-educated, and applied the knowledge learned from legendary boxers and their trainers, to all levels, from the amateur rank to the pro rank, and my intention here is to show you how. If you think by reading so far that I'm wrong, stop! Put down the book and go find a sport where you can be a half-assed trainer, coach or manager and get by. Teach sissy games like football or golf etc., as I am known for saying, the difference between "I can", and "I can't", is apostrophe "t".

Let's turn our focus, let's get to the *science* in boxing that trainers since the late sixties have forgotten. Much has been poorly defined or not defined at all. The first thing a trainer must know, (and I mean MUST know) is what type of fighter you are going to create! Is he going to be a boxer because he doesn't punch hard? Or is he going to be a boxer-puncher, because he has natural ability to do both? Perhaps he's going to be a banger like Marciano, Joe Frazier, Mancini. Or a *smart* banger like Lamata, Archie Moore, or Basilo, to name a few. All these guys were smart fighters! But they fit in one class or another. Because their styles were a reflection of what their trainers and managers knew, we can all benefit and learn from what they had in common: good balance, and a belief in themselves and their styles. Remember, styles make fights.

You'll find as I go along here that much of what I have to tell you about boxing is self-educating. As a boxer, you need to be thinking things out, learning situations, assessing and knowing your opponent. But most of all, you need to know yourself. That is the most important thing you will learn. Most boxing faults come from a lack of knowledge, fear and uncertainty. Tackling those issues boils down to knowing yourself.

In my 13 years as a boxer I went to the ring about 300 times, and every trip was an adventure, where I would store up and recall information on my opponent. I'd be asking: How did he throw his jab? Was he left handed? Did he dance? What kind of angles was he giving me? What about his shoulder feints, head feints? What was his favorite punch? Was it a Hook, Right X-cross or an Upper Cut? Did he move his feet and spin his hips into his punches? Did he step in with his Jab or step to the side when he threw? Did he know what a power zone was? Did he try to end the round with a flurry of punches? Did he try to end the round in his corner and make me walk across the ring at the end of the round? How did he use the referee? Did he step behind him looking for a rest? How well did he take and give body punches? I could go on for hours about the details to note, so these are just some of the things to notice and remember.

Corner People

As a boxer I would rely on my corner people for help. Getting them in the fight is essential, because they let me know what I may or may not be doing to make the fight easier on myself. Knowing the reasons why I was winning or losing made sense, and knowing the difference between winning or losing was the effort. After a fight I would be back at the gym, and practice, practice, practice until I had whatever I didn't have in the last fight. Remember, practice doesn't make perfect, it makes permanent, so if you practice something wrong—guess what? You're screwed! I was a pain in the ass when I was around the old trainers, always looking for something new, always picking their brains with made up situations.

Your Style

Style will depend on your size and strength and will determine how the other guy may try to fight you. You must be able to adapt and adjust accordingly as you go along. You add to what you already know. Make the other guy fight your fight, you can't have any lost motion.

It's not rocket science; it's a matter of being observant, learning through trial and error, picking things up. Watch a video of your opponent, how he warms up, watch his hand movement, his foot movement, how he throws the jab. Does he turn his power hand before he throws it? Where does he hold his hands after he throws combinations? Knowledge is the key to your success. Don't sit around and scratch your ass and pick your nose because it will all get by you and you will probably end up losing more than you'll win. Get the edge any way you can.

Think of ways of neutralizing his jab if he has a good one, observing all of this will amount to a lot of "W" in your column.

Nothing gave me more pleasure than a second chance at the same guy. I never lost to the same guy twice, and beat one guy 4 out of 5 times, that I fought over years. I learned to think all the time when I was in the gym sparring, and went on to do the same in a match. It was not only my physical ability, it was my devotion to practice and concentration on observations that made me excel as a boxer-puncher. Great boxers are not born they are made. A good carpenter doesn't have to aim the hammer every time he strikes the nail. What I mean here is that it's not eyesight so much as it is discipline, knowing when to strike and when to move or duck or dance away.

The Power Zone

I always ask a fighter: how many punches are there in boxing? The answers I get are amazing, one guy told me twenty. I said "name them!", and he stopped after four. *FOUR IS THE MAGIC NUMBER!*

The Jab, Right Cross, Hook, and Upper Cut are the key punches. If you are left-handed: a Left Cross, Right Hook, Right Jab, and an Upper Cut off of your left side. That's right, only four punches, whether you are right or left-handed. This brings us to the power zone.

What is a Power Zone? Get this and get it right: it's the distance that you get with your jab on your opponent without locking your jabbing arm out, or fully extending it. Being able to hit your opponent with your power hand, without reaching for him is critical.

Text for diagrams: Only when you are punching to the head or chest area.

The outside zone is from the top of the head to just slightly under the pectoral muscles of the chest.

Outside Power Zone

This is the area where you should strike when boxing from a distance, or outside.

Inside Zone

So what happens to the zone when you get close or inside on your opponent?

The zone changes from a horizontal position to a vertical position. When you get inside, don't punch from out to in, like the letter C. Punch in an X shape.

Inside or Body Punches

First make sure your knuckles are facing your opponent, palms facing you.

Punch in the letter X going to the liver, lower chest, and stomach, using short hooks—you'll notice I said short hooks and not Upper Cuts. Cross each punch as if you're trying to punch through your opponent's body and come out at his arm pits or spine. You'll find that when you learn how to do this effectively, your opponent will quickly pull back and come into your horizontal zone, and then you can hit him with some good hooks to the head. In this way, your power straight Cross to the head will be much more effective.

The two letter shapes to practice with are: V and X. I'll talk about the letters C *   *   *?? and O later. Work on V and X as much as possible.

90% Mental, 10% Physical

Once you're in excellent shape, boxing is 90% mental and 10% physical. Being smart is the name of the game. "Proper thinking" is more than 90% of effective boxing.

One day I was in the gym earlier than usual, and I went and laid down on the floor next to the ring and was trying mental imaging, when a couple of boxers and their coach walked in and were talking about who was the hardest puncher in the gym. My name came up, and I heard the coach say that when I stopped jabbing from the front heel of my left foot I would become the hardest puncher in the gym, for my weight. It was really funny that everyone in the place seemed to know about me jabbing from the heel of my front (left) foot except me and my coach. I knew then what I had to do: change coaches! I let a few days go by and then I asked my coach, "what's the difference, when I jab or step with the heel of my front foot hitting the canvas first, as compared to using the ball of my front foot first?" He looked at me and said, "there ain't no diff kid!" Needless to say, he was pissed off when I told him I was going to train with someone else.

I started training with the coach that I overheard in the gym a few days before, and the first thing he did was to correct my stance and the angle of my front foot. This is what he taught me: make sure your feet are pointing in the direction that your punches are going. Also, when you jab, make sure your front foot turns out to the left and is as straight as it can be comfortably, and your knee is bent so you don't reach. You'll know if you overturn your foot. Opening your front foot is the key to effective hard punching and it really increases your power by at least 75%. And you'll get better balance. Remember to always step when you jab and turn your front foot counterclockwise for righthanders, and clockwise for southpaws. By doing so it makes your power hand much more effective and now your hook can become dynamite. By turning your front out, it lets you rotate further when you throw power hand behind the jab.

Hip and Upper Body Rotation

A golfer once told a president that you can't hit with authority until you get your ass into the ball. The same applies in boxing. We now get into an area that breeds controversy among trainers that don't know how to instruct a boxer on how to punch. Remember what I said about Williams turning his leg and body and the energy it produced!

Everyone who watched me spar or fight always said that I had great wrist action on the end of my punches, and that's why I punched so hard. Bullshit! The reason I punched hard was that I had learned to keep my knees bent and rotated my hips and upper body towards my target or opponent when I punched with my power hand and left hook. I also rotated my feet in the direction the punch was headed. I always knew it was a gross exaggeration that I had such strong wrists.

Hip rotation is more important in boxing than the actual punch. The way you get your hips and legs into the punch is directly proportional to the power generated. I have never seen a good puncher that didn't have good hip rotation. You would think that it would be an instinctive thing, something picked up in the amateurs. But as I look around at young and even older fighters today and 95% of them don't have any or have very little hip rotation in their punches. Without hip rotation, all you'll ever be is an arm and shoulder puncher, (see diagram) punching outside to in, in a "C" motion.

With your weight evenly distributed over your bent legs, your hips start the rotation. Your back leg knee and foot start to turn, and your shoulder also starts to turn, your arm starts forward, and your forearm start's its turn, as it extends, and finally your wrist snaps over just as you hit your target or the bag or opponent. It's called kinetic energy, which is transferring all that motion and energy onto the end of your fist, through motion! Just like Williams turning on the ball with his bat.

Relaxing
OK! Stop and think: if this is your first time to spar. You are not concerned about mechanics now. Your practice time on the bag or mitts will have made your reactions automatic. If you feel nervous there's nothing wrong with that. Try

to relax and use hand speed with your hips at first until you settle down, which is usually after getting hit once or twice.

If you are so nervous and can't relax, you are going to have a big problem.

Remember a relaxed fighter is the one who can adjust quickly and take care of the business at hand. Your jab is key, if you can't relax right away, jab, jab, jab.

The First Round

My game always started with getting my distance on a guy, with my power zone on the outside first. Once I did that, I started my feints off the jab, looking for the power shot of my right X Cross. Usually early in the first round I would get off a right X Cross to the heart area to see if the guy was in shape. If he sagged a little with a heart shot, I knew he was not in the best of shape and it became a matter of foot work to tire him out while I kept hitting the chest area. If he was in shape, and took the heart shot, then I would get my inside zone and work the body mostly, using head shots also to keep him honest, and to keep him on the defense. But no matter what, I was always looking for heart shots in the first round, no matter what type of fighter he was.

I would also see what he did off of my feints, how he tried to handle my jab and:

- how he moved his feet, his head, his shoulders, his hips
- was he squared up after throwing his punches
- were his knees bent before and after he threw punches
- where was he looking while he punched
- did he or could he adjust to my style
- how well did he fight going backwards, off the ropes, in the corners, in the center of the ring
- did he try to use the ref.
- did he fight for 2 of the judges if there were 3, if there were 5 did he try to fight for them all
- how hard did he hit

I can't impress upon you enough how important the first round of a fight is. It usually sets the tempo for the fight.

Round Two

Corrections and Adjustments

The reason hitting the other guy is tough is that even the best can't get good punches to the target all the time. To do so is a matter of corrections every second, in sparring and in a match. Much of the correction concern is the guy in front of you. A guy who, let's say, is throwing a jab that's flat (see diagram X-X), or is wheeling it in a circle. If he throws it and then drops it as he pulls it back, then you would adjust by throwing a right lead hand or a double right followed by a left hook to the head or body.

If he makes you consistently miss, then you go back to your jab and get your outside zone, or you do a pull in and go to the body. You must think speed and be quick with your feet and shorten the distance between you and your opponent. If you go down to a lower position by bending your knees and he stays up, it's your advantage. Try a jab to the mid-section, followed by a right to the neck or head area, followed by a left hook to the body or head. Keep your knees bent for better balance and quickness.

Try to get him to square up so you get more hitting area or surface to the chest, and stomach area. Remember the best fighters in the history of boxing all had one thing in common: good delivery of their punches. Boxing is 90% from the neck up, and most of what you learn concerns what you do in the gym. It's important to make adjustments, to upset the other guys timing, to throw him off with different motions and angles, shoulder feints and head movement. I'm continually amazed how often fighters don't know these things, as well as most fighters lack the knowledge and intelligence; they aren't smart about the game. Very few fighters know the game between themselves and the other guy. Good fighters and champions are always very observant and constantly thinking three to four moves ahead.

Speed and Punches

There are **3 ways of throwing a jab:**

1. ***Using or starting the jab with your wrist***
   Use this when you want to sneak your power punch in.

2. ***Start the jab from your elbow*** Use this jab when you know you can hook after say, throwing a 1-2 combination.

3. ***From the shoulder*** Use this jab when you know your distance and want to let the other guy know you're in control. Make sure you get your back foot into the punch.

There will be several occasions during the course of a match or sparring session when you should mix up the 3 ways to throw a jab. Practice each way with combinations coming after you use the jab. Multiple jabs from the wrist, elbow and shoulder, combined with shoulder feints and head and foot feints—can really set up your opponent for your best combination to the body and head.

The Cross

Ever wonder why it's called the cross? Nobody today, that I see live or on TV, knows how to properly throw it. I teach it all my guys in the gym. Most trainers I know and have observed, never emphasize its importance, or are able to teach a kid to throw a good Right-Cross. The secret is your feet and hips. But the two most important things are your angle and where you have your power hand. I tell all the people I train that your power hand should be set to strike like a rattlesnake. It does not wind up and then strike, it's already wound up and ready to strike. Just like you should be when you are ready to throw your power punches. If you hold, or have your knuckles facing the floor, before you throw, you will be pushing the punch from the shoulder rather than throwing it and getting your kinetic energy into the punch.

Make sure that when your hands are up, the palms are facing each other if they're not, you will do the following: you'll tend to be squared up giving your opponent more area to hit; you'll tend to punch in the letter "C" rather than a "V"; you'll come up short with your jab; you'll lock out your jabbing hand and probably end up with tennis elbow. Last but not least, don't pull back your jab flat or drop it, because you will be vulnerable to being counter-punched to the neck or head area.

These diagrams will help you with your foot movement and hip rotation. Remember your on-guard position should be at a 25-30 degree angle to your target before throwing any punches. Your head acts as the axis and should not move while throwing combinations or jabs. Your front foot should also point at a 25-30° degree angle from your target before you punch.

Left Hook

Earlier I explained the importance of turning your feet in the direction of your punch. Well let me also explain why you should have your knees bent when throwing your hook. First of all, it gives you more power to the head or body. Secondly, you're not as able to be countered with a right hand or a left hook coming back, because nine times out of ten, your opponent will be above you trying to punch down.

The best left hook I ever saw was when Jersey Joe Walcott knocked out Ezzard Charles for the Heavyweight Title in 1951. Joe Walcott went down and Charles threw a right hand that missed, then Joe brought a short left hook from underneath and hit Ezzard right on the chin and he collapsed, and did not get up for several minutes. Get the video of that fight and study Joe Walcott and Charles, both were tremendous boxers and counter punchers.

Practice the left hook by jabbing straight at you trainer's right mitt or hand, and then jab to his left hand and turn your front foot in the same direction as the punch. You will see how your arm, either left or right, is in the shape of a hook. When you throw a left hook from underneath to the neck or chin area—drive upward slightly, and turn your front foot for more effect.

Learning to throw the hook to the side of the head area

I've helped many pros and amateurs develop a dynamite hook by making them stand in the on-guard position, with their left side for right-handers, or their right side for left-handers, against a wall. I then make then take a short step forward, turning their lead foot and upper body, and throw their hooking arm at either my left or right hand. What the wall does, is to not let you lift your elbow and throw a flat left or right hook. It helps to develop a real snap in your hook. Enrique Annon, who was a great fighter and fought for the World Title, sent his son to me a few years back. When his son went home and showed his father my wall method, he was amazed how well it worked. He commented to his son that he wished that he would have learned to throw a hook from that position. His son later told me that his father was truly amazed at how well he could throw the hook, and the power that he generated for such a small person.

The best left hook artists in my opinion, are Willie Pep, and Willie Pastrano—the Light Heavyweight Champ. They had it down pat. They could throw double and triple hooks with ease, although they were not devastating punches. However they would wear you down in a ten round fight, and knock you on your ass when you least expected it, with their right hand, followed by a solid left hook. I recommend that you get some film or video on these fighters listed below, and watch how they delivered the left hook: Willie Pep, Ray Robinson, Tony Zale, Jersey Joe Walcott, Joe Lewis, Kenny Lane, Joe Frazier, Billy Conn. You should have a ton of fun watching these guys, plus you'll develop a great left hook. Practice, practice, practice until you get it down cold.

Upper Cut
A punch that is very debilitating when used correctly

First let me say that what you see on TV and hear the announcer saying, "He got hit with a short uppercut", is bullshit because there is no such thing as a short uppercut. The upper cut is used only when your opponent is tired and bending or leaning forward, and is only thrown with your power hand.

Kid Gavalan used to throw a Bolo punch, which was a half-uppercut, and semi-effective, but it was only thrown with his arm, and he tried to knock out guys by throwing it to the head or chin area. I really don't know who developed or came up with the uppercut, but when thrown properly, it'd designed to hit you in one of three places: to lower and upper stomach area, the chest, or the head. Picture if you will, a person leaning or bent over. You would bend down slightly from the knees and lean back a little—like a batter getting ready to swing at a pitch—and throw your power hand to the area just above the waistline. If the person tries to lean backward or straighten up, if he sees it coming, you have three shots at hitting him, depending on how far back the person leans or straightens up. Those three places are: the stomach, the chest and the chin area. Always and I mean always, follow the uppercut with a hook.

If you remember Mike Tyson getting knocked out by Buster Douglas in Japan, it all started with an uppercut. Because Mike was getting tired and leaning in when he got hit with it on the chin, followed with a straight left hand from Douglas.

Evander Holyfield knocked out Douglas when he tried to throw an uppercut and missed. Holyfield countered with a right hand, left hook and Douglas's feet and head changed places real quick. So, what's the lesson? Only throw the uppercut when your opponent is tired and leaning over in the center of the ring. Tired is the key word! If he is not tired, and is in the center of the ring and you miss the uppercut, well, lights out for you. Use the uppercut in the corners where your opponent will have a hard time getting away or, on the ropes, and only when he is tired and is not punching effectively enough to hurt you. I can not express enough how important that is. Just picture Mike Tyson trying to pick up his mouthpiece after getting hit by Douglas. Enough said!

I practiced the uppercut in the gym by using a baseball bat, on the heavy bag, and by swinging the bat with my right hand and arm in an upward arc. It worked fine for me. I used it in sparring, at least one round every day, and practiced every day on the Uppercut bag and on the Double End bag. I got hit with it once in one of my early fights, in the chest area and I thought the guy's glove was going to come out my back—it really hurt. I don't know to this day how I ever finished that four rounder. It still hurts 48 years later.

Defense

There is no set defense to use. Every fighter or trainer I've known spend very little time in the gym practicing defense. Willie Pep won a round once without throwing a punch, and he told a reporter, ahead of time, what round it was going to be, and that from making the guy miss, he would come out the next round and knock out the guy. Needless to say I saw the fight on TV, and the ref. stopped the fight in the next round. Willie whipped the guy so badly that it looked like a mismatch, however the other guy was a good fighter with an impressive record.

Let's start with ***the Jab.*** I only know five ways to defend a jab. 1. Catch it with your right hand if you are right-handed, or with your left, if you are a southpaw and are fighting a southpaw. 2. Deflect it. 3. By ducking. 4. By moving your head. 5. By stepping left or right or backwards.

The same with a ***Right or Left cross.*** Catch it with your left hand and deflect with your left hand. Duck, move your head and step away right or left. You could try rolling with the punch by moving your head and shoulders. By using all these techniques in a combination, you should do well.

The ***Left hook*** is by far the most difficult to defend if your opponent is throwing it correctly. This is because it comes from a different angle, to the head or liver area. ***To the head!*:** Block the punch with an open glove on the back of your hand, or duck under! **Do not** try to pull back when it's thrown to your head. Pull in if you can, and let the punch go behind your head. Keep your right glove open as you pull in. ***To the body:*** keep your elbows in tight to your body and bend your knees like you're going to sit down, and block it with your forearm and elbow.

The best defense is a good offense when your opponent is trying to throw a combination. Try to beat him on counter punches to throw him off of his game plan. Remember being in shape is the key to a good defense. Most people don't know how to use their feet and dance away from danger. So staying in shape physically and mentally is essential.*

Defending **_the uppercut_**. If your opponent is hitting you with it, you're in deep shit, or fighting a dumb fight. If you opponent is throwing it from far away or leading with it, just pivot on your left or right foot, and counter punch with your right hand or left hook. I have found that the pivot is about the best defense against a person who is throwing an uppercut from too far away, or doesn't know what he is doing. Good luck.

Defending **_yourself._** Trainers, managers, and corner people are all necessary in helping you, and these people can be your ticket to Easy Street or the Poorhouse, so pick them wisely.

1. Management Team
Find a person who has been in boxing a good length of time and knows the game, the promoters

the Commissioners, and the Sponsors. Pay him his 33.1/3% if he does right by you. If he does not do right by you, drop him as soon as possible. Be aware of the contract you sign with this person, because he will be with you for years. In the State of California you can sign for 1-5 years on a contract. This will vary from state to state.

What I do is this: If a guy comes to me and asks me to train him and be his manager, I suggest that first I become his agent with a Power of Attorney limited to boxing. We'll do a few fights together and get a feel for each other. This way I don't have to waste much time if the guy is a flake and I can walk away without the State Commission being on my case because the fighter was not happy with me. I let the fighter get a taste of what it takes to manage and I let the fighter manage himself with final word on all contracts. I charge 15-30% depending on the fighter.

If I manage the fighter, I insist on at least a three year contract. It will take about that amount of time to get him in contention status for 10 round fights, and possibly World Title fights. Most of all in the end do not manage yourself.

2. The Promotor

Try to fight with names known to the boxing world. Try to get onto good cards when you're starting out in four rounders. This will help you get noticed by other promoters, who may want to use you. Do not sign any promotion deals without a lawyer first looking over the contract. Make sure the lawyers practice is in contract law or specifically in sports contracts. Do not sign with a man who is too buddy-buddy with other promoters. All business should be conducted in a business-like atmosphere. Also do not sign if he has a fighter that is in the same weight class as you.

3. The Trainer

This guy will be your greatest asset or your downfall—the difference between making you a champ or a chump. Remember, earlier in this book I told you about how my trainer said there was no diff. between my heel or the ball of my foot when jabbing. Also remember that I dropped him in a heartbeat. Had I stayed with that guy, chances are good that I would not have had the success nor met the people who made it all happen for me.

Look for a guy who has the answer to your questions, who's been around the game at least 10 years or more. Look at who he's trained and who he is training now. If you have a gut feeling that the guy doesn't know what the hell is going on, then lose him fast. In today's world of boxing, good trainers are far and few between, because boxing has become a secondary sport. People who wish to become trainers drift in and out because of TV. When I was a kid, the three sports were College football, Major League Baseball, and Boxing. Boxing was King because there were thousands of clubs throughout the nation and the world, and it had no season. We used to listen to the fights on the radio, and we would go to the movies and see highlights on the news reels. It was a different time. Fighters used to make a good living and boxing was their job and the had good trainers and managers.

4. The Agent

This guy can also make or break you. Let me start by telling you how the boxing industry works. It works on losers. Think of all the guys and girls that are boxing throughout the world. Ask yourself! How many divisions in boxing? There are about 24 counting the Junior Divisions. So if you take 24 divisons, and take the top 15 guys in each division it comes out to 360 guys including the champs who are winners. The rest have to be losers and never get a shot at the champ. And guess what?! It ain't going to change. So, a good agent gets you the right fights and must know all the right people if he's worth his salt. He should also produce some endorsements for you and commercials advertising of some type of media, and or products advertised on TV.

Remember Marvin Hagler and Archie Moore in the Coca-Cola advertising commercial? Well, they both made more money from that commercial than they did with all the money they made in boxing, at least Archie did. Marvin might have made a little more because he had a mega fight with Ray Leonard.

So pick the right agent, one who's connected to big business, the newspapers and electronic media, and make sure he gets his 15-20% of all your action. Don't be a cheap ass when it comes to this guy.

I would like to leave you with this thought, "boxing is the theatre of the unexpected." It's show business! The key word is business, so treat it accordingly, give back when you can, because you don't get successful without the help from someone. Give and it will come back to you 110%. Boxing is a very corrupt sport with all kinds of crafty and sleazy people. Money is sometimes promised then never delivered. Always insist that everything promised is on paper or in your contract. As my 5th grade teacher Miss Lyesault used to say, "let a word to the wise be sufficient." After all is said and done, the **only person who can make you a champ is you.** You'll have to sacrifice many things, and time, if you want to make it in this sport. I see it day in and day out, I ask, "did you run today?" And I hear:

"I couldn't because it was raining!"

"I got up late".

"I had to have breakfast with my girl!"

"My car broke down and I couldn't get to the track!"

"I forgot!"

On and on, it's all bullshit, and the main reason why so many fail in this sport is that they are not willing to sacrifice what it takes to be successful. It can carry over to their everyday life and the sum total is one word—**loser.**

Contacts

Feel free to contact me at: 7330i@verizon.net

Getting in Shape/ Running

Like a swimmer needs water a boxer needs road work, as in run, run, run, and I don't mean from the bedroom to the kitchen and back to the bedroom to watch TV.

Run uphill as much as you can, do not run downhill facing forward, instead, run downhill backwards and shadow box as you go until you level out again. Pick a distance between telephone poles and sprint, then slow down and jog to next pole, then resume back to a fast pace again. Vary your running speed throughout your runs. *Do not jog for 3 miles—you will not get in fighting shape by merely jogging.*

Note your time for each course you set for your run. If you run a 3 mile course and it takes you, say, 45 minutes the first time, try and cut your time by 2 seconds or better the next time, and then again shave off another 2 seconds the next time and so on. Set a couple of courses with a minimum of 3 miles and a maximum of 20 miles per week. Run: a 3 mile flat course, and a 3 mile course with flat stretches and slight hills; a 4 mile course with flats and slight hills; a 4 mile course with up and down medium hills; a 5 mile course with flats, slight hills and steep hills; and a 10 mile course with all of the above. When you can run the 10 mile course in both directions, you should be in great shape. Remember once you get in running shape, vary your courses and times. Get as close to a 5 or 6 minute mile as you can.

Breathe while you run, so you can get oxygen to your body and avoid getting too tired from the lack of it, and shadow box as you run also. Run in the morning after you get up from a good night's sleep. Don't run after working out in the gym for obvious reasons. Make sure you breathe in lots of air when you're running and when you're sparring, in through the nose and out through the mouth.

Push Ups
At least 300 per week, to start with, increase as you go

Sit ups
At least 600 per week, increase as you go

Shadow Boxing
At least 5 rounds in the ring, at least 3 in the mirror

Skipping Rope
At least 6 rounds per day.

Speed Bag
At least 5 rounds per day—it will help you with speed and keeping your hands up.

Heavy Bag
Use the heavy bag to get strong.

Medium-Heavy Bag
Use this for strength and body punches.

The Wrecking Ball Bag
Use this bag for getting your zone outside and inside. This will help you know when to punch in a "V" or an "X". Do at least double the rounds.

The Judges

Know where the judges are if you're an amateur boxer, because there will be 5 judges. Box near the 2 who are seated next to each other.

The Referees

Most refs are ego maniacs and will always try to get in the act, by telling you different things while you are fighting. Box as clean as you know how and you shouldn't have any problem. Remember most refs are ex-fighters, and tend to tell you how to fight. I knew a ref. who when boxers got close to each other, and it looked like they're holding with one hand, he would say "punch and get out." It's not his job to tell the fighter to punch and get out. If they're holding, he should command break, or stop. If the boxers are using tactics that are against the rules, he should stop the bout, and penalize the boxer or stop the fight.

The ref. is as close to God as any man will ever be while he's in the ring. Some refs will stop a fight too soon, some will give too many warnings, some should not be boxing refs at all. Refs. are supposed to protect the boxers from unnecessary punishment, make sure that the rules are observed, and protect the weaker boxer.

If you're a pro—the refs. work for the State Commission, and if you're over or under-matched, they are on the hook for sanctioning the fight, so for the least reason they have to stop the fight, they will.

In the amateurs it's about the same.

When I fought in New York one time, and I was beating a local favorite, they shut the lights off for a few minutes. When the lights came back on the ref. called the fight a draw.

In England I knocked my opponent down 4 times in 1 round, and the ref. did not stop the fight. The corner people finally stopped the fight after I knocked the guy down 2 more times in the next round. Needless to say the ref. was British and he didn't want to see his countryman lose.

In Spain the ref stopped a fight because I was bleeding from the nose.

I knocked a guy down with a jab and I heard the ref. tell the guy to get up or quit before I picked up the count from the time keeper. There were other incidents that happened throughout my 13 years as a boxer and it always seemed to be in the other guy's home town. I could go on, but I think you get the point.

Thank you for purchasing this book. I hope this manuscript helps to make you a better boxer, and the principles learned from this will enhance your life.

CHART #1

Part A-1:

Give you distance when punching from outside
position and inside position also shows that arms
should be crooked when punching from inside.

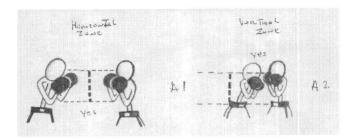

Part B-1:

Shows punching in the letter **V** when outside.
Also B-2 Punching inside using the letter **X** with
arms crooked.

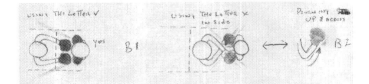

CHART #2

A. Shows punching using the Jab with a slight crook in elbow, shows left hook, shows right cross.

B. Show position of feet when executing each punch.

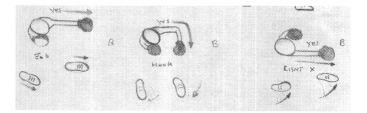

CHART #3

1. Shows how punches should travel when using the letter V. Punching from outside position.
2. Also shows punching in the letter C when in the outside position.
3. Show improper use of jab when returning over to its original position.
4. Shows left jab with slight bend in elbow when hitting target.
5. Show left hook when hitting target.
6. Shows right cross when hitting target with slight bend in elbow when making contact with target.

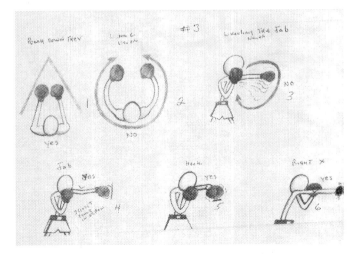

CHART #4

Shows right way to throw a jab.

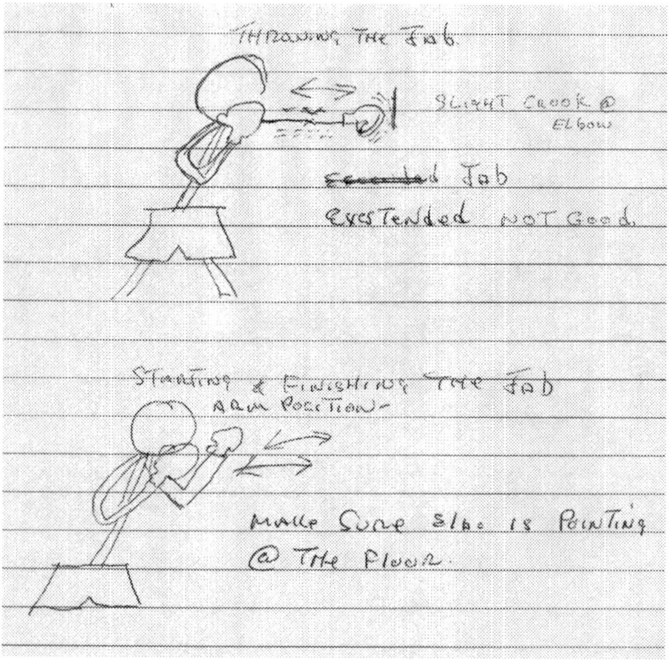

THROWING THE JAB

SLIGHT CROOK @ ELBOW

Extended Jab

EXTENDED NOT Good.

STARTING & FINISHING THE JAB
ARM POSITION —

MAKE SURE ELBO IS POINTING
@ THE FLOOR.

ABOUT THE AUTHOR

Rick Mello boxed from age 10 to 22 as an amateur, boxed mostly in the New England New York area starting in 1945 at local YMCA's, boys club's C.Y.O. (Catholic youth organization) Boy Scouts, the New England street classic and the U.S. Navy. He fought his last bout in South Hampton England with the U. S. Navy. After leaving the navy he decided to turn pro but was injured in an automobile accident. Which injured his back and neck and was advised by doctors not to box. So he took up training Amateur and pro fighters. He moved to the west coast where he established his own Boxing club called (stick & move) an old boxing term he learned as a young boxer. Rick has trained many golden glove champions and state and world champions,,his knowledge of the sweet science is remarkable to say the least. He talks boxing like Ted Williams talked hitting and Willie Pep talked moving.

Printed in the United States
By Bookmasters